WESTERN RIDER

Views from a
Car Window

WESTERN RIDER

CHUCK FORSMAN

with an introduction by William Kittredge
and a conclusion by Gregory Conniff

CENTER FOR AMERICAN PLACES

Santa Fe, New Mexico,
and Harrisonburg, Virginia

PUBLISHER'S NOTES:

This book appears in *The Road and American Culture* series of the Center for American Places,
George F. Thompson, series founder and director. It was issued in a hardcover edition of
2,500 copies, with the generous financial support of the Friends of the Center for American Places.
The publisher and designer, David Skolkin, extend a special acknowledgment to Martha A. Farlow
for her original design concept. For more information about the Center and the publication of
Western Rider: Views from a Car Window, please see page 104.

Center for American Places
P.O. Box 23225
Santa Fe, New Mexico 87502, U.S.A.
www.americanplaces.org

Distributed by the Univeristy of Chicago Press
www.press.uchicago.edu

Library of Congress Cataloging-in-Publication Data is available from the publisher upon request.
ISBN 1-930066-13-9

Frontispiece: "See the U.S.A.," Española, New Mexico

To my parents, Clyde and Lorraine Forsman,
whose love of getting on the road and looking at the world
with childlike wonder has never diminished.

Contents

Prologue

You lean toward the windshield to sense how your future is doing.

—Reg Saner, "Road Life"

Early European settlers were awed and vexed when they saw the American West from wagons and, later, from trains before settling. The word "settlers" is misleading because most didn't stay put very long. Most of us are their spiritual and cultural heirs if not their descendants, and we are still a very unsettled people. This is reflected in our restless mobility and our addiction to cars. The automobile came into widespread use in the West soon after its introduction, and we may be the first culture to virtually grow up with cars. The scale of the Western landscape amplified this dependence — and, for better or worse, helped solidify our identities with cars.

We have breathed auto exhaust all our lives. We wear our cars. We flaunt them; we taunt, swagger, seduce, conceive, and die in them. They reflect our social and marital status, our incomes, recreational inclinations, age, politics, and even our fantasies. We drive to shop, to visit friends, to shuttle kids, to recreate and go anywhere, any time. Besides working, eating, breathing, sleeping, copulating, and consuming . . . we commute. It is the way we live, and the way our parents and grandparents lived before us. We didn't start it and we ride on unaware of where we are taking it (or it is taking us). It has been nearly a century now. It is a part of who we are, and it has also become a part of the way we see.

Western Rider is a compilation of photographs I have taken on the road in recent years from my car. As a landscape painter I spend time traveling simply to look. The difference for me here was in staying in the car and using a camera — and figuring out what this difference meant. In the sequencing of the pictures I attempted to convey the feeling of a journey, even though the narrative is thematic rather than chronological. The pictures themselves and their subjects led me from one to the next, seeking for a telling riddle rather than a conclusion. I remain invisible in all the pictures in order to allow the viewer behind the wheel to reflect a shared experience rather than simply my own.

I first learned to photograph after being drafted and serving as an illustrator in Vietnam in 1968-69. I was soon to become an Army correspondent (photojournalist) as well and traveled extensively, making photographs whose ambivalence reflected my deep aversion to the war. I studied painting in graduate school and learned to use a camera cautiously as a reference tool for my paintings. Still, I continued making photographs for their own sake.

Starting in the mid-1970s I traveled with my wife throughout the forty-eight contiguous states photographing billboards. This was both a response to the billboard removal program of the Highway Beautification Act of 1965 and an examination of American culture for the National Bicentennial in 1976. We mounted an ambitious multimedia exhibition titled "Billbored" but our book project was never published. Later, I made a series of landscape paintings based on views from moving vehicles: cars, buses, airplanes, and motorcycles. I tried to interpret in paintings the way our eyes process movement. I took a lot of photographs for reference but I needed to look hard for myself. I watched along the road and paid attention to my eye movements. They seemed erratic and stuttering— sliding back, then darting ahead as if they were momentarily captured, then released forward again. It was unconscious and swift like the adjustments our pupils make moving in and out of light and shadow or the shifts in focus our eyes make moving from subject to subject. We seem to experience near and far, light and dark, still object and moving object, almost at once.

Yet time is necessary for the swift adjustments that make our seeing functional. The paintings in that series had mixed results. The photographs were merely useful. They captured a single span of time from a single lens with a single focus and aperture. The speed blurs were deceptively smooth while a speed view with our eyes is staggered and irregular. Yet like a rare painting, I found that a still photograph (even a blurred one) can carry its own grace and silent meaning.

Years later, on an overnight drive through Utah, I pulled off the road to look at a dead cow (page 61). I did it to wake up, but it was cold and I stayed in the van and took a picture with the light from my headlamps, then drove on. In my tired state I mused about the dead, bloated cow and wondered about the people in the car or truck that must have hit it. The night was moonless and I wondered what I was missing beyond my blurred, shortsighted tunnel view into the dark. I pondered what it means to look at the world from a car. I thought about the isolation behind a windshield, how framed and fleeting it is, how everything sweeps past but the horizon. In linear perspective, the vanishing point is at the horizon, so by the time the view holds still it vanishes. The car, the road ahead, the signs, the traffic, the dirty air—all diminish the view of places they have already physically violated. Yet it hit me that we see most of the outside world from our cars. Our windshields frame the landscape. Maybe, I thought, in order to understand ourselves better, we should look along our roadways and pay more attention to *the way* we see the world we see. It seemed like a stretch. Still, I considered keeping a camera ready to take photographs from inside the car rather than stopping to take the serious ones outside. I thought of endless reasons why it wouldn't work and why I shouldn't do it. I thought about how tired I was and how foolish this would all seem in the morning. The thoughts accumulated with the miles—and after that these pictures.

Introduction

Highway Vibes
WILLIAM KITTREDGE

A RAGGEDY, HIPPY-MINDED PEACENIK FELLOW told of hitchhiking south across Utah as the sad conflict in Vietnam shuddered to a halt. Facing the deserts beyond Provo at sunset, he took a ride with a hard-handed man in a battered 1956 GMC pickup. A 30-06 rifle hung on the rack inside the rear window.

The details of what came next were not so entirely predictable as we might imagine. Sure, there was the stop for another six-pack, there was the chain-smoking (Camel straights), the drift from no talk at all to muttering monologues concerning bastardly ruination, and the midnight target practice. Way deep in the night, they paused while the driver shot out incandescent lights illuminating commercial roadside signage. At which point my friend asked to be dropped off at the next town.

"Well, it's your problem," the man driving the pickup said. At a lighted off-ramp he pulled over, and stuck out his hand. "Shake," he said.

When that ceremony was finished my friend shouldered his pack and sleeping bag, and headed off to bed down in the brushy night. "Wait a second," the driver said, and he climbed out of the pickup and handed my friend twenty-three dollars.

"You got no choice," the man said. "Traveling broke in this part of the world will land you in jail. Nobody with money would be hitchhiking." So my friend took the money and acted grateful, and in a sort of compromised way he was.

But, compromised or not, the next morning my friend hitchhiked back to Provo, and started south again, rehitching the miles he'd covered with the man in the pickup. "The vibes," he said, "I thought they were so ugly I had to do it over."

This time he caught a ride with a wild-haired grandmotherly woman who talked all the way about gardening in the high valleys of the Unita Range, and about Hungarian cooking, and how she'd grown up among winemakers along the Russian River in California. "Either way," she said, "in the deserts or drinking tea beside the Russian River, you learn. Adversity or sweetness, you learn something. Otherwise you're halfway dead."

By the time she let him off on the outskirts of Las Vegas, my friend was convinced he might himself find a place to set his roots in the coastal valley of the Russian River. So he headed west toward California. "Hadn't been for that first ride," he said, "there would never have been the second one, and I'd never have found myself in Bolinas, where I met my wife. And my daughter, the light of my life, would have never been conceived. That pretty girl wouldn't even exist."

"Vibes," he said, with a big old adoring smile.

Travel stories are usually anecdotal. We go out to renew ourselves, to learn and relearn, and, like any stranger, get most of our learning from glimpses. I began learning to think while driving a pickup truck on my family's ranch in southeastern Oregon. I was put in charge of an expanse of irrigated barley and alfalfa fields despite the fact that I didn't have much idea of how to proceed. I learned on the job, depending on advice I got from hired hands, logging a lot of miles on levee banks, watching and figuring on ways to order the work while wearing out three pickups in eight years.

We all do much of our learning in transit, moving on. In the American West this often works out to watching as we drive by. It's a technique for locating the self in semi-empty vastness, not very intimate with sounds and odors, or the look and feel of textures, more distancing than simple slow-going walking, or, as boys did in my childhood, galloping around on horseback. But, as with montage, there are other rewards—in rapid transit we see sequences, juxtapositions, connections, intimations, and implications that are often not so obvious to those moving at a slower pace.

A pretty girl hanging a roadside thumb (page 52), going where? We sort of know. Going to her life, the rewards and despairs, the fresh loves and raw towns, as Auden wrote, "that we believe and die in." We see it in her lighted face; we see it in the way her friend is struggling to keep up, and in the indifferent surface of asphalt stretching before them.

What we so often see in Chuck Forsman's sequence of roadside photographs is the blurred metaphoric deer in dim light (page 89), nature making its getaway while we pass by (pages 74 and 75), great flapping birds against the sky, flying on, intentions unknown (page 7). Another thing we see is the detritus of our culture, our civilization: worn out agricultural implements lined up on display as if to underline the significance of lives that were worn out while using those tools to impose order onto the fields (page 35). "See, those displays? Say, we were mighty on the earth; we ordered nature."

But all the while we know that manipulation of life on this continent has more than anything else made a mess of things. We know that such arrogance is foolish; we know nature is a field of evolving processes already ordered in ways more complex than we can understand. And we indeed know the profound sadness of the abandoned but carefully placed empty six-pack beside the icebound roadway (page 84). We feel the coldness there, and mourn for our kind and ourselves.

Yet we leaf back to the face of that pretty girl hanging a roadside thumb, on her way toward expectations, full of hope we think, from the way her face is lighted. We yearn to believe in her right to adore life for a while. Chuck Forsman's work is thus a gift. It sustains us and suggests that, while life evolves in ways complex beyond our fathoming, joyousness is still, oftentimes, a reasonable response.

WESTERN
RIDER

Encounter,
Lost River Valley, Idaho

Afternoon of a fawn,
along the Salmon River, Idaho

Eagle leaving road kill,
near Lone Tree, Wyoming

Migrants,
San Luis Valley, Colorado

Pursuit,
I-80, Bonneville Salt Flats, Utah

Desert freight,
southern Idaho

Horizon,
Broomfield, Colorado

Settlement,
I-80, near Rock Springs, Wyoming

City limits,
I-80, Pinole, California

Model home,
Rock Creek subdivision, Superior, Colorado

Housing starts,
Rock Creek subdivision, Superior, Colorado

Native home,
Navajo Indian Reservation, Arizona

Company town,
Lead, South Dakota

18

Copper town,
Anaconda, Montana

High wire act,
Boulder, Colorado

Summer night,
La Grande, Oregon

Street lights,
Loveland, Colorado

Clearing,
Santa Fe, New Mexico

Spark and ice,
a snowplow approaches Albuquerque, New Mexico

Winter diesel,
western Kansas

Lincoln, Kenworth, and Peterbilt,
I-80, between Laramie and Cheyenne, Wyoming

Truck stop,
Miles City, Montana

Cíbola,
Zuñi Pueblo, New Mexico

Glory road,
Miles City, Montana

Prairie Co-op,
Goodwell, Oklahoma

City of Commerce,
with the Denver skyline, Colorado

Machine ages,
Front Range, Colorado

Oil and cotton,
West Texas

Working man, sleeping man,
Boulder, Colorado

Running late,
Denver, Colorado

Before the strike,
Sanford, Colorado

Waiting for green,
Boulder, Colorado

Pulled over,
U.S. 85, Wyoming

Summer boy,
Oregon/Idaho border

Water's edge,
Chief Joseph Dam, Bridgeport, Washington

Summer Eve,
near Banning, California

Couples,
Bodega Bay, California

48

Dust storm at the convenience store,
Green River, Utah

Holy men and Grand Wagoneer,
U.S. 1, northern California

Caution,
Cheyenne, Wyoming

51

Rule of thumb,
State Highway 55, Idaho

52

Reflection,
Navajo lands, Arizona

Shadow dance,
central Wyoming

Incident,
State Highway 99, northern California

Skid master,
Cascade Range, Oregon

57

Cemetery rain,
Anaconda, Montana

Dead of winter,
Northern Cheyenne Indian Reservation, Montana

Milepost,
central Utah

Raven,
Boulder, Colorado

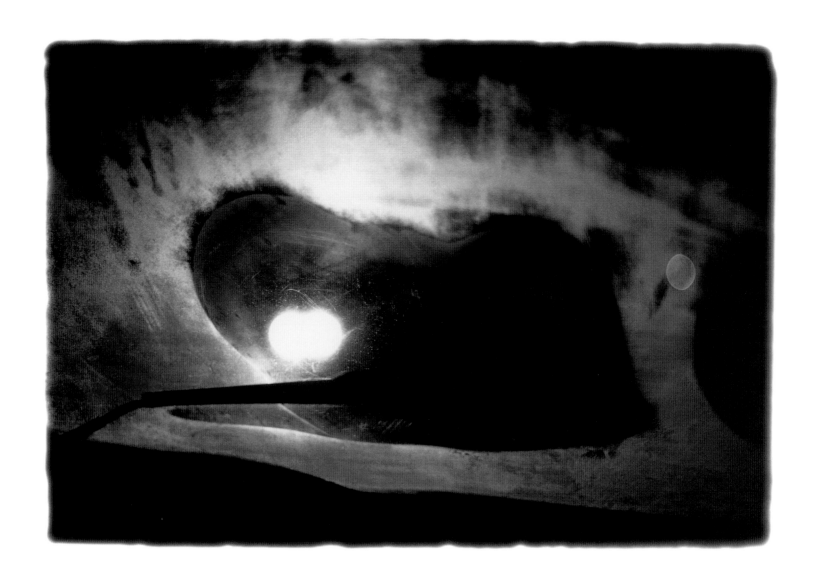

Frost and headlights,
near Soda Springs, Idaho

Carhenge,
near Alliance, Nebraska

Remnants,
Lame Deer, Montana

Monument,
U.S. 89, central Utah

Visitors,
Rapid City, South Dakota

Mountain air,
grocery mural, Arco, Idaho

Night pines and washboard,
near Clear Lake, northern California

Rural density,
near Nederland, Colorado

Heading west,
U.S. 2, eastern Montana

74

Spring hail,
State Highway 24, southern Utah

75

Home stretch,
central Wyoming

Double take,
central Utah

Grey area,
Diamond Mountains, Nevada

Source,
Owyhee Dam, near Adrian, Oregon

Reservoir,
Hells Canyon, Idaho/Oregon border

Across the wide Missouri,
Fort Bertold Indian Reservation, North Dakota

Empty spirits,
Bannock Pass, Idaho/Montana border

School bus,
State Highway 22, North Dakota

Hitchhiker with prairie church,
Pine Ridge Indian Reservation, South Dakota

Mongrel winter,
western North Dakota

Intruders,
near Roundup, Montana

Prairie night,
near Wolf Point, eastern Montana

Vanishing point,
Morenci, Arizona

Blizzard,
U.S. 287, southern Wyoming

Storm,
I-25, central Wyoming

Moving still,
U.S. 14, Wyoming

Conclusion

GREGORY CONNIFF

ANYONE WHO HAS SPENT TIME on the road in the West will recognize in Chuck Forsman's pictures what we see and how we see it when we experience the West by car. His photographs speak the truth to America's enduring but mythic cowboy West. And it is the view from the journey he gives us, not the view from the scenic overlook or the national park. It is what we experience, for example, on the roads between Yosemite and the Grand Canyon and between Yellowstone and the Badlands; or between the airport and our 10,000-acre Montana ranch if we have become rich enough to live far off the highway and away from most of us.

It is the American West at the second millennium; a failed and unpretty dream, but reported here with a poetic directness that is not superior to its subject. There is a huge distance between our dream of the West and the fact of what we have made of it, but Mr. Forsman, born in Idaho, explores this discordant territory with an adult absence of cheap irony or easy anger. His restraint makes him a credible witness without diminishing the boldness or clarity of what and how he sees.

Despite photography's democratic nature and the public character of the highway view, we should not make the assumption that the pictures in this book are the lucky work of a casual eye, or that any of us in the same places could have made the same pictures (a few, perhaps, but not the whole). Mr. Forsman is a painter who for more than thirty years has pursued the subject of the settled Western landscape in large canvases which often show the startling presence of roads. The eye behind his camera lens is an artist's eye; an artist who is gifted, trained, hard-working, and fully alert.

Some of America's strongest photographers have published books about the landscape of the modern West; the best of these coming regularly from Robert Adams, but including also work by Lewis Baltz, Lee Friedlander, and Mark Klett. The American West is the Marilyn Monroe of landscape studies. We will never get over the myth; and good new work will always find a welcome.

Even in this crowd, what this book most calls to mind is Robert Frank's classic mid-fifties work, *The Americans*. One hesitates to write such a thing because Frank's book is the book that changed everything. It showed an outsider's America that was dark, anxious, and shot through with threatening energy and death. It was a gritty immigrant vision free of self-delight and as such it offended many people. Along the way it became a touchstone of truth and inspired some of the best photographic work of the twentieth century while remaining itself an unsurpassed masterpiece.

Based on the energy of his images, Mr. Forsman is an honorable student of *The Americans*. His viewpoint is both unexpected and undeniable. His energy is raw but his aim is true. Yet he possesses what the Swiss-born Robert Frank could not, a native's birthright to a clear-eyed acceptance of America. There is affection in *Western Rider* if not romance.

Mr. Forsman wields his camera with unpremeditated assurance. And he seems to like a challenge. He has chosen to filter a large subject through the structure of a very small formal pattern—the frame of a car window. To complicate his problem he has chosen to work with the heedlessly assembled visual environment which is our lot if we drive this country, even outside the West. Finally, he has made his photographs personal without separating himself from us, his audience, and analytic without distancing himself from the West, his home.

The result is a passionate document, the strongest visual book on the modern American West since Robert Adams turned us towards the subject. *Western Rider: Views from a Car Window* is a terrific body of work that will become more valuable as time goes by. It will open eyes. It has the potential to become a minor classic, and I do not mean that as faint praise.

Acknowledgments

A<small>S THE BUMPER STICKER SAYS</small>, I want to "thank the children," primarily my own. Kids have hungry eyes. Curiosity kills kids and cats alike and it will probably kill me. If my daughters, Chloe and Shannon, egg me on to that end, we may all go out together chasing a glimmer. But my wife, Kris Lewis, being more sensible, keeps us restrained, so I will thank them all for their curiosity and caution (and endurance) which helped see me through this project. I love you all dearly.

My friend Robert Adams was the first photographer to whom I showed the early results of this project. He took it seriously, so I did. He was gracious enough to encourage me and tolerant enough not to remind me that I am primarily a painter. Judgments were always kind, and I agreed with this and didn't with that, and *Western Rider* is not what Bob would have done—it's just much better than I could have done without him. I owe this one to you, and much more, Bob. Thank you.

Another photographer friend, James Balog, provided some of the most candid and helpful critiques of individual pictures that I received. I was buoyed by his enthusiasm for *Western Rider* and the generous attention he gave it. We share an interest in animals, and he probably influenced their prominence in the book. Thanks ever so much, Jim.

A number of others generously shared their time and views on my rough dream. Joellyn Duesberry and Ira Kowal shared valuable input and encouragement at several stages, as did Eric Paddock. Charles Wilkinson, Patricia Limerick, Alex Sweetman, Meridel Rubenstein, Jim Cursley, and Sue Patella provided help in numerous ways.

Others I wish to thank for their generous input are Albert Chong, Jerry West, Frank Rolla, Jeff Limerick, Michael Lichter, Erica Doss, Melanie Walker, Roger Echo-Hawk, Luis Valdovino, Dudley Witney, Bard Martin, Steve Fitch, and David Wrobel.

Special thanks is due George F. Thompson, president and publisher of the Center for American Places, whose openness, patience, critical input, and support of this project were indispensable.

About the Photographer and the Essayists

Chuck Forsman was born in 1944 in Nampa, Idaho, and he was raised in Oregon and California. He received his B.A. and B.F.A. in art (painting) at the University of California, Davis, and he learned photography while serving in Vietnam as an illustrator and correspondent. Among Mr. Forsman's numerous honors are three grants from the National Endowment for the Arts and an American Academy of Arts and Letters Award. His first book of paintings, *Arrested Rivers*, was published by the University Press of Colorado in 1994. Mr. Forsman has had more than forty solo exhibitions since 1971, including shows at the Gerald Peters Gallery in Santa Fe, New Mexico, Tibor de Nagy Gallery in New York City, the Nevada Museum of Art, the Tucson Art Museum, and the Wichita Art Museum. His work is in the permanent collections of the Colorado Springs Art Center, Denver Art Museum, Hallmark Cards in Kansas City, Missouri, Knoxville Museum of Art, Metropolitan Museum of Art in New York City, Phoenix Art Museum, Princeton University Museum of Art, Wichita Art Museum, Yellowstone Art Museum in Montana, and Chase Manhattan Bank in New York City. Mr. Forsman is a professor of fine arts and painting at the University of Colorado, Boulder.

William Kittredge was born in 1932 in Portland, Oregon, and he was raised on the MC Ranch in Adel, Oregon. He is a professor of English at the University of Montana, and the author or editor of more than a dozen books, including *Southwestern Homelands* (National Geographic, 2002), *The Nature of Generosity* (Knopf, 2000), *The Portable Western Reader* (Penguin, 1997), *Hole in the Sky: A Memoir* (Knopf 1992), *The Last Best Place: A Montana Anthology* (Montana Historical Society, 1990), and *Owning It All* (Graywolf, 1987). He resides in Missoula.

Gregory Conniff was born in 1944 in Jersey City, New Jersey, and he grew up in Montclair, New Jersey. He practiced law until 1978 when he devoted his life full-time to photography and writing. His books include *Common Ground* (Yale, 1985) and *Gregory Conniff: Twenty Years in the Field* (Sordoni Art Gallery, 1999). His photographs have been exhibited widely and are part of numerous collections, including the Art Institute of Chicago, Center for Creative Photography in Tucson, Corcoran Gallery of Art in Washington, D.C., High Museum of Art in Atlanta, Museum of Modern Art in New York City, and San Francisco Museum of Modern Art. He resides in Madison, Wisconsin.